Key Stage 2
Maths
Addition, Subtraction, Multiplication & Division

NAPE
National Association for Primary Education

Contents

AUTHOR: Camilla de la Bédoyère
EDITORIAL: Catherine de la Bédoyère, Quentin de la Bédoyère, John Bolt, Vicky Garrard, Kate Lawson, Sally MacGill, Julia Rolf, Lyndall Willis
DESIGN: Jen Bishop, Dave Jones, Colin Rudderham
ILLUSTRATORS: David Benham, Sarah Wimperis
PRODUCTION: Chris Herbert, Claire Walker
Thanks also to Robert Walster

COMMISSIONING EDITOR: Polly Willis
PUBLISHER AND CREATIVE DIRECTOR: Nick Wells

3 book Pack ISBN 1-84451-053-0   Book ISBN 1-84451-030-1
6 book Pack ISBN 1-84451-066-2   Book ISBN 1-84451-081-6
First published in 2003

A copy of the CIP data for this book is available from the British Library upon request.

Created and produced by
FLAME TREE PUBLISHING
Crabtree Hall,
Crabtree Lane,
Fulham, London SW6 6TY
United Kingdom
www.flametreepublishing.com

Flame Tree Publishing is part of The Foundry Creative Media Co. Ltd.

© The Foundry Creative Media Co. Ltd, 2003

Printed in Croatia

Foreword

Sometimes when I am crossing the playground on my way to visit a primary school I pass young children playing at schools. There is always a stern authoritarian little teacher at the front laying down the law to the unruly group of children in the pretend class. This puzzles me a little because the school I am visiting is very far from being like the children's play. Where do they get this Victorian view of what school is like? Perhaps it's handed down from generation to generation through the genes. Certainly they don't get it from their primary school. Teachers today are more often found alongside their pupils, who are learning by actually doing things for themselves, rather than merely listening and obeying instructions.

Busy children, interested and involved in their classroom reflect what we know about how they learn. Of course they learn from teachers but most of all they learn from their experience of life and their life is spent both in and out of school. Indeed, if we compare the impact upon children of even the finest schools and teachers, we find that three or four times as great an impact is made by the reality of children's lives outside the school. That reality has the parent at the all important centre. No adult can have so much impact, for good or ill, as the young child's mother or father.

This book, and others in the series, are founded on the sure belief that the great majority of parents want to help their children grow and learn and that teachers are keen to support them. The days when parents were kept at arm's length from schools are long gone and over the years we have moved well beyond the white line painted on the playground across which no parent must pass without an appointment. Now parents move freely in and out of schools and very often are found in the classrooms backing up the teachers. Both sides of the partnership know how important it is that children should be challenged and stimulated both in and out of school.

Perhaps the most vital part of this book is where parents and children are encouraged to develop activities beyond those offered on the page. The more the children explore and use the ideas and techniques we want them to learn, the more they will make new knowledge of their very own. It's not just getting the right answer, it's growing as a person through gaining skill in action and not only in books. The best way to learn is to live.

I remember reading a story to a group of nine year old boys. The story was about soldiers and of course the boys, bloodthirsty as ever, were hanging on my every word. I came to the word khaki and I asked the group "What colour is khaki?" One boy was quick to answer. "Silver" he said, "It's silver." "Silver? I queried. "Yes," he said with absolute confidence, "silver, my Dad's car key is silver." Now I reckon I'm a pretty good teller of stories to children but when it came down to it, all my dramatic reading of a gripping story gave way immediately to the power of the boy's experience of life. That meant so much more to him, as it does to all children.

JOHN COE
General Secretary
National Association for Primary Education (NAPE).

NAPE was founded 23 years ago with the aim of improving the quality of teaching and learning in primary schools. The association brings together parents and teachers in partnership.

NAPE, Moulton College, Moulton, Northampton, NN3 7RR, Telephone: 01604 647 646 Web: www. nape.org.uk

Maths: Addition and Subtraction, Multiplication and Division is one of six books in the **Learn** series, which has been devised to help you support your child through Key Stage Two.

The National Curriculum gives teachers clear guidelines on what subjects should be studied in Mathematics, and to what level. These guidelines have been used to form the content of both this book and **Shape, Size and Distance**, the accompanying maths text in this series.

Each page contains exercises for your child to complete, an activity they can complete away from book and **Parents Start Here** boxes to give you extra information and guidance. At the end of the book you will find a checklist of topics — you can use this to mark off each topic as it is mastered.

This book has been designed for children to work through alone; but it is recommended that you read the book first to acquaint yourself with the material it contains. Try to be at hand when your child is working with the book; your input is valuable. The teaching of mathematics has changed since you were at school and you may find you can learn something useful too!

Encourage good study habits in your child:
- Try to set aside a short time every day for studying. 10 to 20 minutes a day is plenty. Start each learning session with two minutes spent on mental maths; your child will be used to doing this at school.
- Establish a quiet and comfortable environment for your child to work and provide scrap paper, sharp pencils, a rubber and a ruler. A calculator is required to complete the book.
- Give your child access to drinking water whenever they work; research suggests this helps them perform better.
- Reward your child; plenty of praise for good work motivates children to succeed.
- Ensure your child eats a healthy diet, gets plenty of rest and lots of opportunity to play.

This book is intended to support your child in their school work. Sometimes children find particular topics hard to understand; discuss this with their teacher, who may be able to suggest alternative ways to help your child.

Top Tip!
If your child struggles with anything, don't worry – let them go at their own pace.

Parents Start Here!

Your child needs to know place value up to 1000, but many children love big numbers and enjoy learning about numbers up to a million.

Numbers can be big or small, but they are all made up of digits.

Putting Numbers In Their Place

These are the digits we use: **0 1 2 3 4 5 6 7 8 9**

Draw a circle around the 2-digit numbers and a square around the 3-digit numbers. One of each has been done for you.

18   (23)   19   495   8

2809   304   90   1

999   6   81   295

It is important to put your digits in the right order. Writing our digits in columns like these can help.

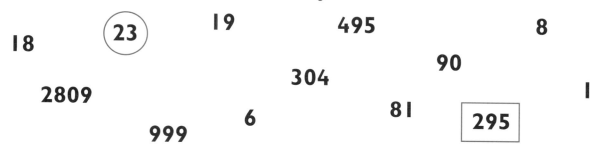

thousands	hundreds	tens	units
5	2	1	8

The number here is 5218

there are 8 units (or 'ones')

there is 1 ten

there are 2 hundreds

there are 5 thousands.

Put these numbers in to the columns. Start with the units.

904   **1236**   **59**

4

If you have numbers that look similar, it can be hard to know which one is bigger: 978, 789, 897.

These numbers all have hundreds, tens and units.

Look at the number of hundreds and then you can put them in order:

7 hundreds   **8** hundreds   **9** hundreds

7 8 9 ⟶   **8 9 7** ⟶   **9 7 8** ⟶   BIGGER

Number lines also help us put numbers in to the right order. Look at this number line and put the missing numbers into the boxes.

140   **150**   ☐   ☐   **180**   **190**   ☐   **210**   ☐   **230**

When you know what the digits mean you can add, subtract, multiply or divide numbers. You can also write their names out:

124 = one hundred and twenty four

3468 = three thousand four hundred and sixty eight

78 690 = seventy eight thousand, six hundred and ninety

Home Learn

Put these numbers in order, starting with the smallest.

(10 000) (990) (578) (67) (89 729) (9724) (587) (34)

Activity

Write down some 3, 4 and 5 digit numbers. Now see if you can write down their names.

Check Your Progress!
Putting Numbers In Their Place ☐
Turn to page 48 and put a tick next to what you have just learned.

Parents Start Here!

Set your child some addition problems with more 3-digit numbers and carrying over into the hundreds column. Watch them as they work through the problems, prompting them to follow all the steps.

Adding Numbers

Let's think about adding the numbers **132** and **56**

Step one: Think about the sum. Make a guess: this sum is about 130 + 55, which equals 185.

Step two: Write it down. The digits must be in the right place. Make sure your units are lined up in a column. If it helps, write the names of the columns to remind you. Put the biggest number at the top. Draw the plus sign and the answer lines.

hundreds	tens	units
h	t	u
1	3	2
5	6
1	8	8

⟵ write your answer here

Step three: Add the units. 2 + 6 = ? Put the answer at the bottom of the units column.

Step four: Add the tens. 3 + 5 = ? Put the answer in the tens column.

Step five: Add the hundreds. There is only 1 hundred – easy! This needs to go in the hundreds column.

Step six: Check your answer. Is your answer close to 190? If there's a mistake, this is when you will spot it.

It's quite likely you could have reached the answer, 188, without writing it down, but look at this sum, which is a bit harder:

157 + 26 =

Step one: Think about the sum and put your rough answer here ☐

Step two:

```
    1   5   7
+       2   6
_____
_____
```
plus sign ——→
answer lines ——→

put the tens here   put the units here

Step three: 7 + 6 = 13

You can not put two digits into one column so put the 3 into the units column and carry over the 10 into the tens column.

```
    1   5   7
+       2   6
_____
            3
_____
        1
```

Step four: Adding all the tens: **5 + 2 + 1 = 8**

add all the tens

```
    1   5   7
+       2   6
_____
    8   3
```

Step five: Add the hundreds

Step six: Did the final answer match your rough answer? If not, check your adding and your rough answer.

```
    1   5   7
+       2   6
_____
1   8   3
```

Home Learn

Do the following sums. Set them out properly before you start.

123 + 45 =

347 + 24 =

801 + 149 =

Activity

Tell your parents how you add up in your head. See if they are as good at it as you are.

Check Your Progress!
Adding Numbers

Turn to page 48 and put a tick next to what you have just learned.

Parents Start Here!

Adults use estimation and rounding-off all the time. Let your child get involved in measuring and weighing at home or in the grocers. Ask them to estimate the measurements or weights first.

Estimation And Rounding

On the last pages you learned that you had to think about a sum before you even started adding to get a rough answer. In your head you were making a sensible guess.

The word we use for making a sensible guess is estimating.

We estimate when we are going to check that an answer to a sum is correct, or when the exact answer doesn't matter.

Here is a sum that we can estimate:

76 + 27 =

We know that the two numbers are very close to 75 and 25

We know that **75 + 25 = 100**

So we can estimate that the answer will be about 100.

We can then work out the exact answer by putting the numbers into columns:

$$\begin{array}{r} 7\ 6 \\ +\ 2\ \ 7 \\ \hline 1\ 0\ 3 \\ 1 \end{array}$$

or we can see that
76 is 1 more than 75
and 27 is 2 more than 25

so we can add the differences to 100 to get our answer

100 + 1 + 2 = 103

We can see that our estimate was very close to the exact answer – it was a good estimate.

When we don't need an exact answer, we use a number close to it. Sometimes we even know the exact answer, but it is more useful to find an easier number it is close to. This is called rounding off. We round off to the nearest ten or hundred or thousand.

If you are going to round off a number, you need to decide whether you should round it up or down. Unless you have a good reason, you should round it to the closest 10 or 100. (You will always be told what you should round to.)

If you are rounding to the nearest 10, and your number ends in a 5, you should round it up.

A number line can help:

13 is closer to 10, so round down

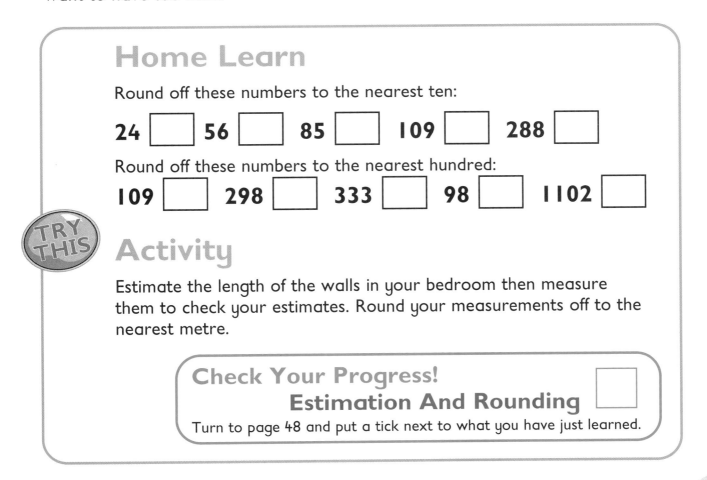

round to the nearest ten
answer: 10

round to the nearest ten
answer: ☐

round to the nearest hundred
answer: ☐

Look at this example:

Patty needs 24 cm of string, but the shop only sells it in units of 10 cm.
Why does she buy 30 cm?

Because 24 is closer to 20 than to 30, we would normally expect her to round down to 20 cm, but in this case we have to round up, because Patty doesn't want to have too little.

Home Learn

Round off these numbers to the nearest ten:

24 ☐   56 ☐   85 ☐   109 ☐   288 ☐

Round off these numbers to the nearest hundred:

109 ☐   298 ☐   333 ☐   98 ☐   1102 ☐

TRY THIS

Activity

Estimate the length of the walls in your bedroom then measure them to check your estimates. Round your measurements off to the nearest metre.

Check Your Progress!
Estimation And Rounding
☐
Turn to page 48 and put a tick next to what you have just learned.

Top Tip!
Remember to give your child lots of praise – they'll work so much better.

Parents Start Here!

It is useful to recognise the subtractions which involve carrying over. Obviously if no carrying over is necessary, it is more likely your child will be able to work out the answer mentally.

Subtracting Numbers

Subtraction means taking away.

Subtracting numbers is the opposite of adding.

274 – 52 =

You can subtract in your head, or you can write the numbers down to work the sum out.

Estimating is a good idea whether you are doing a sum on paper or in your head

Step one: Think about the sum. Make an estimate of what the answer might be. If you think about it being

270 – 50 =

does this makes it easier to estimate?

Step two: make sure the units are lined up

h	t	u
2	7	4
–	5	2

put the biggest numbers on the top

Step three: Subtract the units

h	t	u
2	7	4
–	5	2
		2

start with the units
$4 – 2 = 2$

put the answer in the units column

Step four: Subtract the tens

h	t	u
2	7	4
–	5	2
	2	2

subtract the tens
$7 – 5 = 2$

put the answer in the tens column

Step five: Subtract the hundreds

h	t	u
2	7	4
–	5	2
2	2	2

subtract the hundreds
$2 – 0 = 2$

put the answer in the hundreds column

Step six: Check your answer. Is the answer close to your estimate? If not, did you make a mistake in your estimate, or in the subtraction?

Now let's try a harder subtraction, with some carrying-over.

$$674 - 125 =$$

Step one: Think about the sum and estimate an answer.

Step two: Write out the sum

```
  h  t  u
  6  7  4
- 1  2  5
_____
```

Step three: Subtract the units

```
  h  ⁶t  ¹u
  6  7̶  4
- 1  2  5
_____
        9
```

but you can not take 5 away from 4, there aren't enough units.

We need to change one of the tens in to 10 units. This leaves 6 tens and 14 units.

put the answer in the units column $14 - 5 = 9$

Step four: Subtract the tens

```
  h  ⁶t  ¹u
  6  7̶  4
- 1  2  5
_____
     4  9
```

$6 - 2 = 4$

put the answer in the tens column

Step five: Subtract the hundreds

```
  h  ⁶t  ¹u
  6  7̶  4
- 1  2  5
_____
  5  4  9
```

$6 - 1 = 5$

put the answer in the hundreds column

Step six: Think about the sum again and check your answer against your estimate.

Home Learn

Try these subtractions. You may find that you can do some of them in your head. Use another piece of paper if you need to.

876 − 437 =   89 − 66 =   347 − 128 =   111 − 106 =   880 − 73 =

Activity

Ask a grown-up to set you a subtraction that involves carrying the units and the tens. Can you solve it?

Check Your Progress!
Subtracting Numbers

Turn to page 48 and put a tick next to what you have just learned.

Top Tip!
Don't worry if your child does not understand straightaway – children learn at different speeds.

Parents Start Here!

Encourage your child to play shop with real money and fixed prices, it is not only useful for everyday life, but also an excellent introduction to decimals.

Money Numbers

When we write about money we have three special symbols.

£   this symbol is called a pound sign.

.   this symbol looks like a dot. It is called a decimal point. It separates the pounds from the pence.

p   this is the letter 'p' and it is short for pence.

There are 100 pence, or pennies, in one pound.

This book costs three pounds.
We write it like this: **£3.00**

This pencil costs fifty pence.
We write it like this: **50p**

This packet of pens costs two pounds and ninety nine pence.

We write it like this: **£2.99**

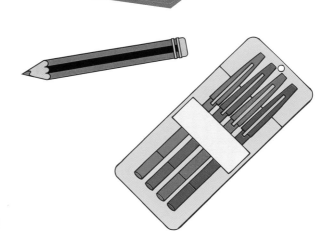

When there are pounds we do not write the 'p', we just use the pound sign.

When there are no pounds we just use the pence symbol 'p'.

Adding and Subtracting Money

When you add or subtract money you do the sum in just the same way as any other addition or subtraction.

But remember to put in the decimal point.

Example:

Add £6.23 and 57p

put in the decimal point

put the pound sign into the answer

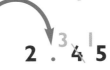

```
  £ 6 . 2 3
+     . 5 7
  £ 6 . 8 0
          1
```

Example:

Subtract 26p from £2.45

put in the decimal point

put the pound sign into the answer

```
      3  1
    2 . 4 5
  -   . 2 6
  £ 2 . 1 9
```

Home Learn

Paul has been given nine pounds fifty for his birthday. He buys a kite for four pounds ten pence and an aeroplane for three pounds ninety nine. Work out how much of his birthday money he has spent. How much money does he have left?

working out box

answer

Activity

Next time you spend £1.00, estimate how much change you will get back. Do the subtraction in your head, and work out the change.

Check Your Progress!
Money Numbers

Turn to page 48 and put a tick next to what you have just learned.

13

Activities

Addition Tables

1. Complete this addition table. Some of the numbers have been put in for you.

+	3	4	5	6	7	8
5						
6			11			
7	10				14	
8						
9				15		
	10			15		

> to work out 6 + 5, run one finger along ——— the 6 row
> and another finger down the 5 column. They meet at the answer, 11

Here is a grid for you to make your own addition table. Put your own numbers along the top and the side. Use some numbers that are bigger than 10.

+						

Money Problems

When you are solving money problems you must remember to keep the numbers in their columns and the decimal point in the right place.

2. Write the totals next to the shopping baskets

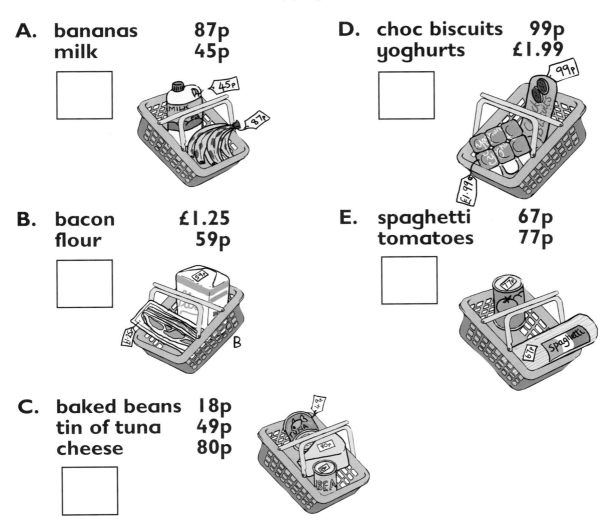

A. bananas   87p
     milk   45p

D. choc biscuits   99p
     yoghurts   £1.99

B. bacon   £1.25
     flour   59p

E. spaghetti   67p
     tomatoes   77p

C. baked beans   18p
     tin of tuna   49p
     cheese   80p

3. Monty had been collecting Pikaplum cards since his last birthday. He has now got 7345. Monty is planning to sell 1200 cards, which are doubles, to his friend Mikey. How many will he have left?

Mikey already has 923 Pilaplum cards. How many will he have once he has bought Monty's doubles?

15

Top Tip! If your child loses concentration here, let them take a break.

Parents Start Here!

Children now learn their Times Tables up to ten, not twelve. However, it will help if you encourage them to try and work out their tables beyond this limit. If your child finds it impossible to learn their tables you should discuss this with their teacher – it may be symptomatic of problems with number recognition and learning.

Introducing Multiplication

There are 4 lots, or groups, of pigs in this pen. You can find out how many pigs there are by:

Counting them one at a time: 1, 2, 3, 4, 5, 6, 7, 8. This works, but it would take a long time if you were trying to count 50 pigs.

Counting them in groups of two. The pigs are standing in groups of two, so you can count them using your two times table:

2, 4, 6, 8

Counting in groups is a faster way of counting big numbers, and that's all that multiplication is.

We can say there are 4 lots of 2 pigs, or 4 times 2 pigs, or best of all we can write it using the symbol x, which means times or multiplied by:

4 x 2 = 8

The pigs have moved around the pen. Now there are 2 groups of 4 pigs.

There are the same number of pigs, they have just arranged themselves in a different way.

We can write it like this:

2 x 4 = 8

Remember: it doesn't matter which way round you write a multiplication – the answer is always the same. Think of the pigs!

Times Tables

We are going to look at multiplying more numbers, but before we do, there is something you have to know:

You MUST MUST MUST learn the Times Tables.

We will be going through the 2, 10, 5, 3 Times Tables in some detail in this book, and that will help you to learn them.

Here is a Times Tables square. It has got all of the Times Tables in it up to 10. You can look back at this when you need a reminder and you can also use it to start learning the other Tables – off by heart!

To use the Times Tables square run one finger along a row and another finger down a column until they meet.

×	1	2	3	4	5	6	7	8	9	10
1	1	2	3	4	5	6	7	8	9	10
2	2	4	6	8	10	12	14	16	18	20
3	3	6	9	12	15	18	21	24	27	30
4	4	8	12	16	20	24	28	32	36	40
5	5	10	15	20	25	30	35	40	45	50
6	6	12	18	24	30	36	42	48	54	60
7	7	14	21	28	35	42	49	56	63	70
8	8	16	24	32	40	48	56	64	72	80
9	9	18	27	36	45	54	63	72	81	90
10	10	20	30	40	50	60	70	80	90	100

Home Learn

Use the Times Table square to find the answers to these multiplications:

a) 7 x 2 = ☐

b) 6 x 3 = ☐

c) 5 x 10 = ☐

d) 8 x 5 = ☐

e) 9 x 4 = ☐

Activity

Make your own Times Tables square and stick it somewhere in your house where you are likely to see it often (like the bathroom). Now you can test yourself every day and you'll soon know your tables off by heart.

Check Your Progress!

Times Tables ☐

Turn to page 48 and put a tick next to what you have just learned.

Top Tip!
If your child struggles with anything, don't worry – let them go at their own pace.

Parents Start Here!

The method of division using a number line is called 'repeated subtraction'. It is useful until your child has a reasonable knowledge of the Times Tables and can start tackling short and long division (pages 38 and 48).

Looking At Dividing

Dividing is the opposite of multiplying.
Dividing is the same as sharing. It is important when you share or divide that everything is shared equally.

Lucy has been told to share a packet of 12 sweets with her brothers:

Lucy's share: Tim's share: Mike's share:

Is this fair? Whose share would you rather have?

If Lucy shares the sweets out again, fairly. How many sweets should they get each? ☐

Let's use the same numbers to make a multiplication:

3 lots of ☐ sweets equals 12

3 × ☐ = 12

You can divide by using a number line:

On this number line you are jumping backwards. Each time you jump back, you are taking away 3. The number line shows how 21 is divided into 7 groups of 3.

We use this sign ÷ to show divided by or shared by. **21 ÷ 7 = 3**

We say: 21 divided by 7 is 3 or 15 shared by 5 is 3 or 5 goes into 15 3 times.

There is another way to write divisions too: 3 ←the answer is written on top

the number we are dividing by goes here ↗ $7 \overline{)21}$ ↖put the big number inside

Remember the 8 pigs on page 16? They could stand in 4 groups of 2, or 2 groups of 8

$8 \div 4 = 2$ $8 \div 2 = 4$

That's right – you can also write the division both ways. Just remember to leave the big number alone, or you'll get very confused!

Roger the Rat was tidying away his shoes. He put 10 in the top rack, and 10 in the bottom rack. But Roger found he had one left over.

So that means Roger had 21 shoes in total. The division looks like this:

$21 \div 2 = 10 +$ 👟

Remainder is the word for left over. You can't always draw it, so you should use the sign 'r' or the word 'remainder' – whichever your teacher prefers you to use. The division now looks like this: $21 \div 2 = 10 \ r1$

Or you can write it like this: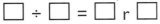
$$\begin{array}{r} 2 \ r1 \\ 10\overline{)21} \end{array}$$

Home Learn

Turn these problems into divisions. Use the Times Table Square to help you work them out. The first one has been done.

1. I share 24 biscuits between 8 biscuit tins. $24 \div 3 = 8$
2. 45 buns were shared between 9 elephants. ☐ ÷ ☐ = ☐
3. There were 5 cars and each of them had 4 people inside.
☐ ÷ ☐ = ☐
4. I had 25 socks, which made 12 pairs with 1 left over.
☐ ÷ ☐ = ☐ r ☐

Activity

Use the number table on pages 24–25 like a number line to work out how to work out how you would share a big packet of 50 sweets between you and two of your friends. Would there be a remainder?

Check Your Progress!
Looking At Dividing
Turn to page 48 and put a tick next to what you have just learned.

Parents Start Here!

Top Tip! Go through this page as often as you like until your child understands it fully.

Once your child is confident of the 2 Times Table get them to start manipulating the numbers. Ask them what you multiply by 2 to get the answer 28 etc.

The Two Times Table

Kelly the Kangaroo is jumping along the number line. She is jumping in groups of 2.

1 2 3 4 5 6 7 8 9 10 11 12 13 14 15 16 17 18 19 20 21

We write the multiplication like this: **4 x 2 = 8**

The numbers that Kelly lands on are all multiples of 2. They can be divided by 2 without having any left over, and are known as even numbers.

The multiples of 2 are just the numbers in the 2 Times Table.

This is the 2 Times Table:

1 x 2 = 2	**5 x 2 = 10**	**9 x 2 = 18**
2 x 2 = 4	**6 x 2 = 12**	**10 x 2 = 20**
3 x 2 = 6	**7 x 2 = 14**	
4 x 2 = 8	**8 x 2 = 16**	

Multiplying by 2 is the same as doubling.

100 is double 50, or it is twice 50.

Dividing by 2

When you divide any number by two, you are sharing equally between 2. This is the same as halving the number:

These 10 butterflies have been divided into two groups. There are 5 butterflies in each group. Half of 10 is 5.

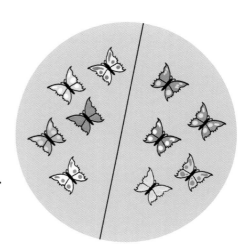

The division looks like this: **10 ÷ 2 = 5** Or this:

$$2{\overline{)10}}\,^{5}$$

Dividing by 2 is easy because halving is easy.

Try these divisions:

27 ÷ 9 = ☐

3)30 = ☐

18 ÷ 2 = ☐

2)42 = ☐

Numbers that have a remainder when you divide them by 2 are called odd numbers.

Home Learn

Complete the following, including any remainders:

100 ÷ 2 = ☐

50 ÷ 2 = ☐

51 ÷ 2 = ☐

☐ **x 2 = 22**

☐ **÷ 2 = 6 r1**

Activity

Put this book away, stand up and recite the 2 Times Table. You can't sit down again until you can get all the way up to ten, without a single mistake! But can you carry on any further?

Check Your Progress!
The Two Times Table ☐

Turn to page 48 and put a tick next to what you have just learned.

21

Parents Start Here!

As soon as your child starts dividing with larger multiples of 10, they are likely to be faced with decimals. Remind them how you write pounds and pence, and, unless they feel confident, try to keep to 2 decimal places.

The Ten Times Table

Kelly the Kangaroo is jumping along the number line in multiples of 10.

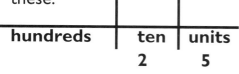

1 2 3 4 5 6 7 8 9 10 11 12 13 14 15 16 17 18 19 20 21 22 23 24 25 26 27 28 29 30 31 32 33 34 35 36 37 38 39 40

We write the multiplication like this: **4 x 10 = 40**

Look at the number line and write down some more multiples of ten:

☐ ☐ ☐ ☐

When we learned about adding numbers together we put the numbers into columns like these:

hundreds	ten	units
	2	5

When we multiply by 10 we are making a number 10 times bigger. This means each digit moves one place to the left and a zero fills the space.

This works with bigger numbers too:

When we are multiplying by 100 we are making a number 100 times bigger. This means the digits move two places to the left and 2 zeros fill the space

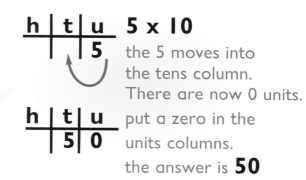

5 x 10

the 5 moves into the tens column. There are now 0 units.

put a zero in the units columns.

the answer is **50**

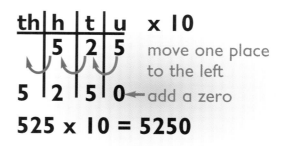

x 10

move one place to the left

add a zero

525 x 10 = 5250

move 2 places to the left

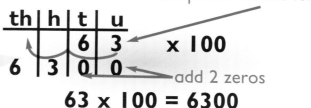

x 100

add 2 zeros

63 x 100 = 6300

Dividing by 10

We know that multiplying and dividing are opposites, and when we multiply by 10 we add a zero and move the digits to the left. Can you guess what we do to divide by 10?

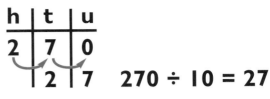

$$270 \div 10 = 27$$

Yes, it is that easy! All you have to do is take away a zero and move the digits one place to the right.

Try these divisions:

$$980 \div 10 = \boxed{} \qquad 60 \div 10 = \boxed{}$$

$$10\overline{)70} \qquad\qquad 10\overline{)180}$$

Roger the Rat is having a party and he is sorting out the party bags for his guests. He has bought 42 lollies, and has 10 bags for his 10 guests. He shares the lollies out but there are some left over. Write the division:

$$42 \div \boxed{} = \boxed{} \text{ remainder } \boxed{}$$

If you were Roger, what would you do with those left over lollies?

Home Learn

Ben wants to plant some rows of vegetables in his allotment. He wants it to look neat, so decides to plant 10 vegetables to a row.

a) Ben plants 6 rows of carrots. How many carrots is that altogether? $\boxed{}$

b) He plants 120 cabbages. How many rows is that? $\boxed{}$

c) If Ben wanted 10 times the number of potatoes as cabbages, how many potatoes would he want? $\boxed{}$

Activity

Find out how you multiply and divide by 1000.

Check Your Progress!
The Ten Times Table $\boxed{}$

Turn to page 48 and put a tick next to what you have just learned.

Top Tip! Remember to give your child lots of praise – they'll work so much better.

Parents Start Here!

Now is the time to really consolidate what your child has learned about multiplication and division so far. Set your child lots of simple problems and guide them slowly through the steps.

The Five Times Table

This is the 5 Times Table:

1 2 3 4 5 6 7 8 9 10 11 12 13 14 15 16 17 18 19 20 21 22 23 24 25 26 27 28 29 30 31 32 33 34 35

1 x 5 = 5	3 x 5 = 15	5 x 5 = 25	7 x 5 = 35	9 x 5 = 45
2 x 5 = 10	4 x 5 = 20	6 x 5 = 30	8 x 5 = 40	10 x 5 = 50

On this number square colour in all the multiples of 5 (all the way up to 100) in yellow, and draw a red circle around the numbers in the 10 Times Table.

Look at the pattern and the numbers. What do you notice? Fill in the gaps:

The numbers in the 5 Times Table all end in a ☐ or a ☐ .

The numbers in the 10 Times Table all end in a ☐ .

Did you notice that the answers in the 10 Times Table are double those in the 5 Times Table?

1	2	3	4	5	6	7	8	9	10
11	12	13	14	15	16	17	18	19	20
21	22	23	24	25	26	27	28	29	30
31	32	33	34	35	36	37	38	39	40
41	42	43	44	45	46	47	48	49	50
51	52	53	54	55	56	57	58	59	60
61	62	63	64	65	66	67	68	69	70
71	72	73	74	75	76	77	78	79	80
81	82	83	84	85	86	87	88	89	90
91	92	93	94	95	96	97	98	99	100

Look: **3 x 10 = 30**   **3 x 5 = 15**

15 is half of **30**   **30** is double **15**.

If you want to multiply something by 5, you can multiply by 10 and then halve the answer.

Divide by 5

When you divide by 5 you are sharing equally between 5. Draw rings around groups of 5:

How many groups are there?

If there had been 17 ladybirds, how many would have been left over? [   ]

There is another easy way you can divide by 5. Simply divide by 10 then double the answer:

$$80 \div 5 = \;?$$

Divide by 10: $80 \div 10 = 8$

Double the answer: $8 \times 2 = 16$

So $80 \div 5 = 16$

Home Learn

a) $20 \times 5 =$ [   ]   b) $90 \div 5 =$ [   ]   c) $12 \times 5 =$ [   ]

d) $80 \div 5 =$ [   ]   e) $60 \div 5 =$ [   ]

Activity

See if you can work out a way of doing the multiplication 8×50. Clue: if you multiply by 8×5, you only have to do a simple multiplication to reach the answer.

Check Your Progress! [   ]
The Five Times Table
Turn to page 48 and put a tick next to what you have just learned.

25

Top Tip!
Don't worry if your child does not understand straightaway – children learn at different speeds.

Parents Start Here!

There is no short cut to dividing by three so emphasis must be put on learning the 3 Times Table, which requires lots of repetition. You can make it more interesting by asking your child questions that require them to manipulate the numbers.

The Three Times Table

Kelly the kangaroo is jumping along her number line in 3s. Can you draw in the bouncing arrows, to take her up to number 24?

1 2 3 4 5 6 7 8 9 10 11 12 13 14 15 16 17 18 19 20 21 22 23 24 25 26 27 28 29 30

This is the 3 Times Table:

1 x 3 = 3	3 x 3 = 9	5 x 3 = 15	7 x 3 = 21	9 x 3 = 27
2 x 3 = 6	4 x 3 = 12	6 x 3 =18	8 x 3= 24	10 x 3 = 30

Here is a clever thing to know about the 3 Times Table. If you add up the digits in the multiples of 3, they always add up to another multiple of 3.

12 gives us the sum 1 + 2 = 3

15 gives us the sum 1 + 5 = 6

18 gives us the sum 1 + 8 = 9

Now go back and check where your bouncing arrows landed. Add the digits and check if they are all multiples of 3.

Now you can multiply by 3, and multiply by 10 or 100 you could multiply by 30 or 300.

Let's try and do this multiplication: **30 x 4**

All you have to do is multiply 3 x 4, then multiply the answer by 10.

4 x 3 = 12 ⟶ **12 x 10 = 120**

Now try to multiply **300 x 5**

Remember: to multiply by 100 move the digits 2 places to the left and add 2 zeros.

3 x 5 = ☐ ⟶ **☐ x 100 = ☐**

Divide by 3

Dividing by 3 is easy because now we can recognise multiples of 3, we know whether there will be a remainder or not.

Mr Pearce is planning to take 21 boys on scout camp to Appleby Farm. Three boys can fit in a tent. Mr Pearce will be staying in the farmhouse, but how many tents does he need to take for the boys?

$$2 + 1 = 3 \text{, so } 21 \text{ is in the 3 Times Table}$$

$$3 \times 7 = 21$$

$$\text{so } 21 \div 3 = 7$$

He needs 7 tents.

If there were 22 scouts, we would have the division

$$22 \div 3 = 7 \text{ r}1$$

Mr Pearce would need to take 8 tents or they wouldn't all fit in.

Home Learn

Mrs Campbell has three children: Charley, Louis and Dylan. To avoid arguments, she is always very careful that they get equal shares of everything. Here is what she bought for their Christmas stockings:

9 micro-robots

19 stickers

33 chocolate coins

17 felt-tip pens

What does Louis have in his stocking on Christmas day?

_____

What has Mrs Campbell kept back, to avoid arguments?

_____

Activity

See if you can write down three 6-digit numbers that are multiples of 3. Can you write the numbers in words?

> ### Check Your Progress!
> **The Three Times Table**
> Turn to page 48 and put a tick next to what you have just learned.

Activities

1. There are 5 Minty Spangles in each packet. How many Minty Spangles do Polly, Jack and Keisha have each?

Polly   **Jack**   **Keisha**

Polly has [ ] mint spangles

Jack has [ ] mint spangles

Keisha has [ ] mint spangles

2. Are these statements true or false? Tick the box.

825 is a multiple of 3 and a multiple of 5.   True [ ]   False [ ]

275 is a multiple of 3 and a multiple of 5.   True [ ]   False [ ]

All numbers that end in 0 are multiples of 5.   True [ ]   False [ ]

A number divided by 5 is half the size of the same number divided by 10.   True [ ]   False [ ]

3. This number line shows Kelly the Kangaroo jumping in groups of 100. Put the missing numbers in:

300   400   600   900   1000

4. Mina is rabbit monitor at school. She feeds Percy the rabbit each playtime at school, once in morning break, once in the lunch break and once in afternoon break, from Monday to Friday. Mrs Feldman looks after Percy at the weekends.

How many times does Mina feed Percy in one week?

working out box

answer [ ]

The bag of rabbit food contains 300 servings. How many days does it last?

working out box

answer [ ]

5. Penny has 80p to spend in the shop.

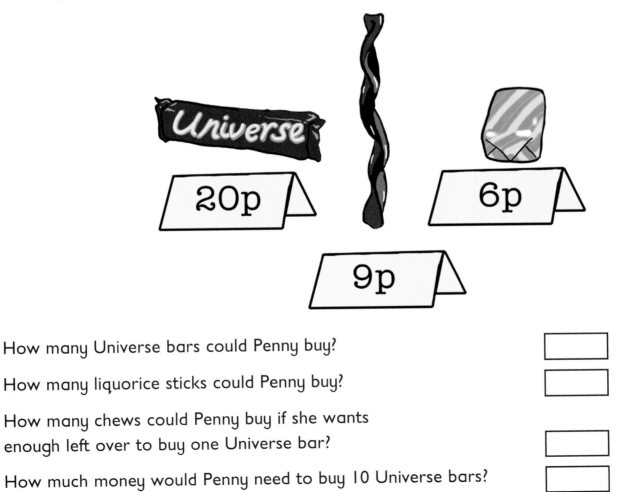

Universe 20p   9p   6p

How many Universe bars could Penny buy? [ ]

How many liquorice sticks could Penny buy? [ ]

How many chews could Penny buy if she wants
enough left over to buy one Universe bar? [ ]

How much money would Penny need to buy 10 Universe bars? [ ]

Top Tip!
Learning is fun, so if your child is tired, let them come back to this when they are fresh.

Parents Start Here!

The better you know your Times Tables, the easier you will find it to multiply and divide big numbers.

More Times Tables

2, 4 and 8 Times Tables

Colour in all the multiples of 2 in yellow

Put a red ring around all the multiples of 4

Draw a blue dot by the all multiples of 8

Complete the following sentences:

All the multiples of 8 are also multiples of ☐ and multiples of ☐.

The answers in the ☐ Times Table are double those in the 2 Times Table. That is because ☐ is double 2.

The answers in the 8 Times Table are ☐ those in the 4 Times Table.

1	2	3	4	5	6	7	8	9	10
11	12	13	14	15	16	17	18	19	20
21	22	23	24	25	26	27	28	29	30
31	32	33	34	35	36	37	38	39	40
41	42	43	44	45	46	47	48	49	50
51	52	53	54	55	56	57	58	59	60
61	62	63	64	65	66	67	68	69	70
71	72	73	74	75	76	77	78	79	80
81	82	83	84	85	86	87	88	89	90
91	92	93	94	95	96	97	98	99	100

9 Times Table

Use the number square above to write down all the multiples of 9:

9	☐	☐	☐	☐
☐	☐	☐	☐	90

Can you see that the units go down 1 each time you add 9, and the tens go up 1 each time?

Now add the digits of each number. You always get 9 or a multiple of 9.

Also, because 9 is a multiple of 3, all the digits add up to a multiple of 3, too.

Here's another trick with the 9 Times Table:

If you can't remember 8 x 9, think of it as 9 lots of 8.

This is the same as 10 lots of 8 minus 1 lot of 8

8 x 10 = 80

80 − 8 = 72

so **8 x 9 = 72**

The easiest route to the answers, though, is to learn them off by heart.

Write out the 11 times table. It has got a great pattern; it is the easiest table to learn!

Home Learn

Complete the following. Try to work out the answers before checking them in the Times Table Square on page 17.

3 x ☐ = 21   9 x 4   = ☐

6 x 7   = ☐   6 x ☐ = 24

☐ x 9   = 81

Activity

Write out the 7 Times Table. Ask a grown up to help you play Fizz Buzz. You each take it in turns to count, starting at 1. Whoever gets to a multiple of 5 must say 'fizz' instead of the number. Whoever gets to a multiple of 7 must say 'buzz' instead of the number. Why must you say 'fizzbuzz' instead of 35?

Check Your Progress!

The Four, Eight And Nine Times Tables

Turn to page 48 and put a tick next to what you have just learned.

Top Tip! If your child loses concentration here, let them take a break.

Parents Start Here!

The real strength in this method is that it enables children to understand what they are multiplying before they attempt long multiplication by columns – which we tackle next.

Multiplying Some Bigger Numbers

Here is a problem that needs some BIG multiplying:

Colin is a teacher. He buys 31 packets of felt-tip pens for his class. There are 14 pens in each packet. How many pens did Colin buy?

This is what the multiplication looks like: **31 x 14 = ?**

Here is one way to work this out, it's called the Grid Method:

Step one: Draw a grid. Put a cross in the top left hand corner

Step two: Take the first number and separate it into tens and units 31 is the same as 30 and 1 unit Put these across the top of the grid

x	30	1
10		
4		

Step three: Take the second number and separate it into tens and units 14 is the same as 10 and 4 units. Put these down the side of the grid

Step four: You can now do each bit of the multiplication.

$30 \times 10 = 300$
$4 \times 30 = 120$

x	30	1
10		
4		

$10 \times 1 = 10$
$10 \times 1 = 10$

Step five: Your grid now looks like this, and you can begin to add the numbers together.

$\begin{array}{r} 300 \\ + 120 \\ \hline 420 \end{array}$

x	30	1
10	300	10
4	120	14
	420	14

$10 + 4 = 14$

Step six: Your final step is to add the two totals:

$\begin{array}{r} 420 \\ + 14 \\ \hline 434 \end{array}$

Let's do another.

The multiplication looks like this: **46 x 12 = ?** Make your estimate before you begin. Try 46 x 10 to get a rough answer.

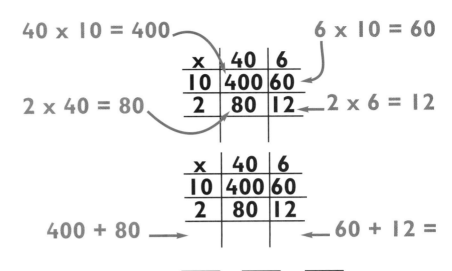

40 x 10 = 400

6 x 10 = 60

2 x 40 = 80

2 x 6 = 12

x	40	6
10	400	60
2	80	12

The multiplications have been done for you, now you can do Step 5 – adding the columns together.

x	40	6
10	400	60
2	80	12

400 + 80 ⟶

⟵ 60 + 12 =

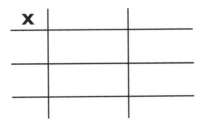

Now you can do **Step Six** – add your totals:

+

Finally, check your answer and compare it with your estimate.

Home Learn

Use the grid method to solve the multiplication 51 x 38

x		

Activity

Make up your own multiplications and solve them using this method.

Check Your Progress!
Multiplying Some Bigger Numbers
Turn to page 48 and put a tick next to what you have just learned.

Parents Start Here!

Do not expect your child to have got to grips with long multiplication after this introduction. View this section as an opportunity for you to brush up on the topic so you can teach your child.

Multiplying In Columns

Let's look again at Colin the teacher. He had 31 packs of 14 pens. We will do the same multiplication but by a different method.

Step one: Put the bigger number at the top. Line up the units.

$$\begin{array}{r} 3\,1 \\ \times\ 1\,4 \\ \hline \end{array}$$

Step two: Multiply the units in the bottom row by the units in the top row and put the answer in the units column.

Now multiply the units in the bottom row by the tens in the top row and put the answer in the tens column.

$4 \times 3 = 12$

$$\begin{array}{c c c} \textbf{tens} & \textbf{units} \\ 3 & 1 \\ \times\quad 1 & 4 \\ \hline 1\quad 2 & 4 \\ \end{array}$$

$4 \times 1 = 4$

Step three: Multiply the top row by the tens on the bottom row. But before you can do that you must put a zero in the units column.

$$\begin{array}{c c c} \textbf{tens} & \textbf{units} \\ 3 & 1 \\ \times\quad 1 & 4 \\ \hline 1\quad 2 & 4 \\ \end{array}$$

put the zero here ⟶ **0**

Step four: Multiply the tens in the bottom row by the units in the top row and put the answer in the tens column.

Now multiply tens in the bottom row by the tens in the top row and put the answer in the hundreds column.

$1 \times 1 = 1$
$1 \times 3 = 3$

$$\begin{array}{c c c} & \textbf{tens} & \textbf{units} \\ & 3 & 1 \\ \times & 1 & 4 \\ \hline 1 & 2 & 4 \\ 3 & 1 & 0 \\ \hline \end{array}$$

Step five: Add the two totals

$$\begin{array}{c c c c} & \textbf{tens} & \textbf{units} \\ & 3 & 1 \\ \times & 1 & 4 \\ + & 1\quad 2 & 4 \\ & 3\quad 1 & 0 \\ \hline & 4\quad 3 & 4 \\ \end{array}$$

Don't panic if that seemed hard. Try the same multiplication using the grid method and it might help you to see exactly what you were doing.

Now let's try another:
I have 27 aliens visiting me. They each have 16 hands and I have promised to knit them some gloves because they don't like our cold weather. How many gloves do I need to knit?

27 x 16 = ?

Step one: Look carefully at this stage – there are too many digits to fit into the units column so you have to carry 4 tens over.

carry over the 4
put the units in
the units column

7 x 6 = 42

```
    t   u
    2   7
x   1  ₄6
        2
```

Step two:

6 x 2 = 12

12 + 4 = 16

```
    t   u
    2   7
x   1   6
1   6   2
```

put the answer here

Step three: Remember to put a zero in the units column.

```
    t   u
    2   7
x   1   6
1   6   2
2   7   0
```

1 x 2 = 2

1 x 7 = 7

put the answer here

put a zero in the units column

Step four: Add the totals together.

```
    t   u
    2   7
x   1   6
+1  6   2
 2  7   0
 4  3   2
    1
```

Which method of multiplying did you prefer? Sometimes the grid method is quicker, sometimes the columns method is quicker, that is why you will need to learn both.

Check Your Progress!
Multiplying in Columns
Turn to page 48 and put a tick next to what you have just learned.

Activities

215

60   **36**   **150**   **38**   **20**   **135**

25   **81**

1.   From the numbers above, write down the multiples of:

5 _____

4 _____

9 _____

3 _____

Check your answers using a calculator.

2.   Callum is collecting stickers for his sticker book. They cost 22p each and he needs 36 stickers altogether.

How much money it will cost Callum to fill his sticker book?

working out box

answer [   ]

3.   Estimate the answers for the following multiplications. Put a tick by the number you think is closest.

a) 35×23 = ? 700 [ ]   7000 [ ]   800 [ ]   8000 [ ]

b) 22×22 = ? 50 [ ]   300 [ ]   500 [ ]   4000 [ ]

c) 105×38 = ? 150 [ ]   1500 [ ]   2000 [ ]   4000 [ ]

4. There are 70 pupils in Year 3 at Byrne School: 24 in class 3a, 21 in class 3b and 25 in class 3c.

Mr Lee is organising a quiz. Each class needs to be organised into teams of 6. If there are any pupils left over, they can join existing teams to make teams of 7.

How many teams of 6, and how many teams of 7 in each class? If you find this difficult then work it out using counters, buttons or coins to represent the pupils.

Class 3a: [   ] teams of 6 and [   ] teams of 7

Class 3b: [   ] teams of 6 and [   ] teams of 7

Class 3c: [   ] teams of 6 and [   ] teams of 7

working out box

5. Simon has a full pack of 52 playing cards. He deals all the cards out to himself and his three friends.

a) How many does each person have?

working out box

answer [   ]

b) Are there any cards left over?

working out box

answer [   ]

Top Tip!
If your child struggles with anything, don't worry – let them go at their own pace.

Parents Start Here!

Let your child be entirely confident about everything they have covered so far before introducing the other method of division, long division. A confused child will quickly lose interest in maths.

Short Division

When we looked at dividing we found that we could write divisions like this:

$$2\overline{)6\ 8\ 2}$$

We say six hundred and eighty two divided by two.

To work this division out you just have to divide each digit inside the box by the number outside. Always start from the left.

1. 2 goes into 6 3 times. Put the 3 above the 6

3. 2 goes into 2 1 time. Put the 1 above the 2

$$\begin{array}{c} 3 \quad 4 \ \text{r}1 \\ 2\overline{)6\ 8\ 2} \end{array}$$

2. 2 goes into 8 4 times. Put the 4 above the 8

The answer is **341**.

You can check your divisions by multiplying them back again:

341 x 2 = 682

Let's try that again. We will do this division:

936 ÷ 4 = ? We write this as: $4\overline{)9\ 3\ 6}$

Start at the left.

put the 2 here ⟶ **2**

$$4\overline{)9\ {}^1\!3\ 6}$$

9 ÷ 4 = 2 r 1

and the remainder goes here

$$2\ 3$$
$$4\overline{)9\ {}^13\ {}^16}$$

$13 \div 4 = 3\ r\ 1$

put the 6 here and the remainder here

Now you can divide the units.

$$2\ 3\ 4$$
$$4\overline{)9\ {}^13\ {}^16}$$

$4 \times 4 = 16$ exactly

put the 4 here. There are no remainders.

Check your answer:

We know that 4 x 250 is 1000 – so this looks like a sensible answer. Now multiply it back to be sure:

4 x 234 = 936

Home Learn

Try these divisions:

a) 546 ÷ 3 = ☐

b) 670 ÷ 5 = ☐

c) 984 ÷ 6 = ☐

d) 917 ÷ 7 = ☐

working out box

Activity

Your brain is probably buzzing right now. Put away the book, go outside and run about until you've got rid of that terrible buzzing and HAVE A BREAK! You've earned it.

Check Your Progress!
Short Division ☐

Turn to page 48 and put a tick next to what you have just learned.

Top Tip!
Go through this page as often as you like until your child understands it fully.

Parents Start Here!

Go through the steps slowly. There is nothing difficult here, but it needs concentration to put the right bits in the right place. Make up more sums without remainders; they are more satisfying to solve.

Long Division

When the divisions use bigger numbers, we can't use short division, but we can still work it out without using a calculator.

Look at the sum **3236 ÷ 14**

Step one: Write the sum as if we were going to use short division.

$$14 \overline{)3\ 2\ 3\ 6}$$

Step two: Start from the left. How many times does 14 go into 3? It doesn't! So try it with the next digit as well.

How many times does 14 go into 32? It goes 2 times. Put the 2 on the top row, above the other 2.

Step three: Multiply your answer by the 14.

2 x 14 = 28. Put this under the 32 and subtract it to get 4. This is the remainder.

This is where you would notice if you had divided 14 into 32 correctly. If our remainder was not between 0 and 14, we would know we'd made a mistake.

$$
\begin{array}{r}
2 \quad\quad \longleftarrow 32 \div 14 \text{ goes 2 times} \\
14 \overline{)3\ 2\ 3\ 6} \\
-\ \ 2\ 8 \quad \longleftarrow 2 \times 14 = 28 \\
\hline
4 \quad\quad \longleftarrow 32 - 28 = 4
\end{array}
$$

Step four: Now move on to the next digit, 3. Drop it down by the remainder to make 43.

How many times does 14 go into 43? It goes 3 times. Put this in the top row, above the 3.

Now multiply 3 x 14 = 42. Put this under the 43 and subtract to get 1.

$$
\begin{array}{r}
2\ 3 \\
14\overline{)3\ 2\ 3\ 6} \\
-\ 2\ 8 \\
\hline
4\ 3 \\
-\ 4\ 2 \\
\hline
1
\end{array}
$$

43 ÷ 14 goes 3 times

3 x 14 = 42

43 – 42 = 1

Step five: Now for the final digit, 6. Drop it down to make 16.

How many times does 14 go in to 16? It goes one time. Put this on the top row, above the 6.

Now multiply 1 x 14 = 14. Put this under the 16 and subtract to get 2. This is your final remainder.

The answer to that very long division is **231 r2.**

$$
\begin{array}{r}
2\ 3\ 1 \\
14\overline{)3\ 2\ 3\ 6} \\
-\ 2\ 8 \\
\hline
4\ 3 \\
-\ 4\ 2 \\
\hline
1\ 6 \\
-\ 1\ 4 \\
\hline
2
\end{array}
$$

16 ÷ 14 goes 1

1 x 14 = 14

16 – 14 = 2

Home Learn

Write down the 23 times table from 23 to 230

Use another piece of paper for this question, as it will take up quite a lot of space!

Activity

Use your 23 times table to work out the long division 6325 ÷ 23.

If you end up with a remainder, you have gone wrong somewhere.

Check Your Progress!
Long Division
Turn to page 48 and put a tick next to what you have just learned.

Top Tip!
Learning is fun, so if your child is tired, let them come back to this when they are fresh.

Parents Start Here!

Practise sharing things out at home using the terms third, fifth, eighth and so on. Share out large numbers and single items to show that fractions are not only used for parts of 1, but also for dividing groups.

Introduction To Fractions

We have learned how to divide numbers. Can you divide 1 up?

Yes, you can, if that 1 is a cake:

1 cake has been cut into 8 pieces.

1 cake has been divided between 8 people.

1 has been divided by 8. We write it like this $\frac{1}{8}$. This is called a fraction.

or if that 1 is a bar of chocolate:

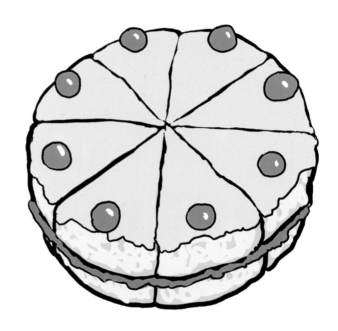

Fill in the numbers:

☐ bar of chocolate has been cut into ☐ pieces

☐ bar of chocolate has been divided between ☐ people

☐ has been divided by 10. We write it like this:

$$\overline{10}$$

This is called a fraction.

Here are some other fractions you have already come across at school:

One half $\frac{1}{2}$

One quarter $\frac{1}{4}$

Two quarters is the same as one half $\frac{2}{4} = \frac{1}{2}$

Colour in one third $\frac{1}{3}$ of this circle.

We know that when we halve a number, we divide it by 2.

$$\frac{1}{2} \times 10 = 5 \text{ or } 10 \div 2 = 5$$

When we want to find a third of a number, we divide it by 3.

$$\frac{1}{3} \times 12 = 4 \text{ or } 12 \div 3 = 4$$

Can you work out what a quarter of **24** is?

Home Learn

colour in $\frac{1}{4}$ ⟶

colour in $\frac{1}{3}$ ⟶

colour in $\frac{1}{5}$ ⟶

colour in $\frac{1}{8}$ ⟶

Activity

Take a large piece of square paper and fold it in half, then half again. Keep folding in half until you can't fold any more. How many folds could you make? Try this experiment again, with different sized pieces of paper. What do you discover?

Check Your Progress!
Introduction To Fractions
Turn to page 48 and put a tick next to what you have just learned.

Activities

1. Estimate the nearest answer to these divisions. Put a tick by the number you think is closest.

a) **325 ÷ 2 = ?**   60 ☐   100 ☐   150 ☐   300 ☐

b) **1500 ÷ 25 = ?**   1300 ☐   120 ☐   80 ☐   60 ☐

c) **180 ÷ 15 = ?**   5 ☐   10 ☐   15 ☐   20 ☐

2. Fill in the gaps in this long division.

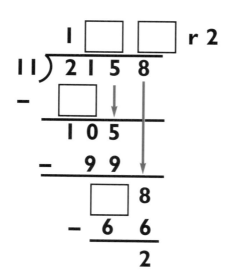

3. St Peter's School is having a football tournament and everyone in Year Four wants to play. There are 112 pupils. How many teams of 11 are there?

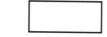

a) How many pupils are left over?

b) Every Year Four pupil is given a quarter of an orange at half time. How many oranges are needed?

4. Mr Patterson has made 720 pork pies for the local supermarket.

a) There are 4 pies in each pack. How many packs does Mr Patterson have?

working out box

answer [   ]

b) Mr Patterson can fit 10 packs into one box. How many boxes does he need?

working out box

answer [   ]

c) Mr Patterson can fit 9 boxes into the boot of his car. How many times will he have to drive to the supermarket to get all the pork pies delivered?

working out box

answer [   ]

Circle Of Seven

Follow the instructions around the circle and see if you can come back to the number of 7. If you don't, you've made a mistake somewhere. You can do your working out anywhere on the page.

Once you've got it right, go back the other way, but swap x for ÷, + for − etc.

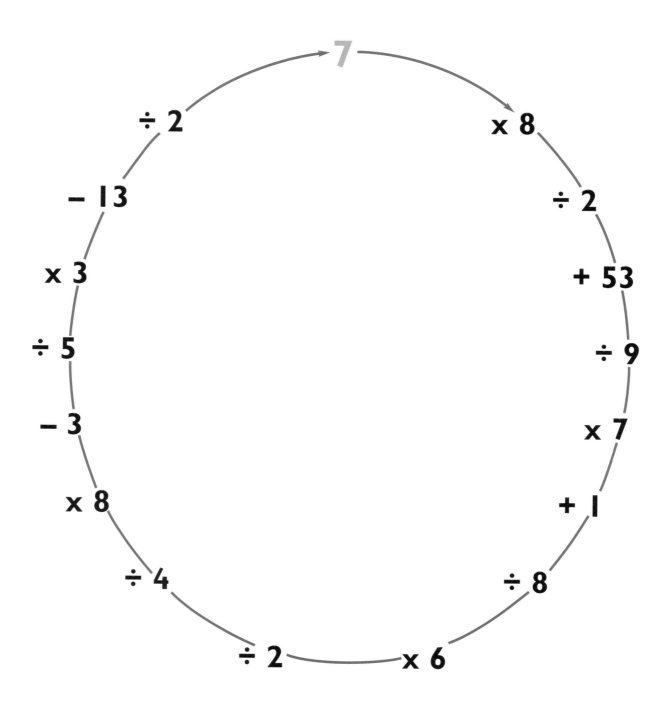

Answers

Pages 4–5
The 2 digit numbers are:
18, 19, 23, 81, 90
The 3 digit numbers are:
295, 304, 495, 999
Units:
9 0 4
1 2 3 6
5 9
Number line:
140 150 160 170 180 190 200 210
220 230
Home Learn
34 67 578 587 990 9724 10 000
89 729

Page 7: Home Learn
123 + 45 = 168
347 + 24 = 371
801 + 149 = 950

Page 9: Home Learn
24 = 20
56 = 60
85 = 90
109 = 110
288 = 290
109 = 100
298 = 300
333 = 300
98 = 100
1102 = 1100

Page 11: Home Learn
876 − 437 = 439
89 − 66 = 23
347 − 128 = 219
111 − 106 = 5
880 − 73 = 807

Page 13: Home Learn
Paul has spent £8.09
(£4.10 + £3.99)
He has £1.41 left (£9.50 − £8.09)

Pages 14–15
1.

+	3	4	5	6	7	8
5	8	9	10	11	12	13
6	9	10	11	12	13	14
7	10	11	12	13	14	15
8	11	12	13	14	15	16
9	12	13	14	15	16	17
10	13	14	15	16	17	18

2. Money:
A = £1.32
B= £1.84
C= £1.47
D = £2.98
E= £1.44
3. Monty:
Monty will have 6145 cards left
(7345 − 1200).
Mikey will have 2123 cards
(923 + 1200).

Page 17: Home Learn
a) 7 x 2 = 14
b) 6 x 3 = 18
c) 5 x 10 = 50
d) 8 x 5 = 40
e) 9 x 4 = 36

Page 19: Home Learn
Buns: 45 ÷ 9 = 5 or 45 ÷ 9 = 5
Cars: 20 ÷ 5 = 4 or 20 ÷ 4 = 5
Socks: 25 ÷ 2 = 12 r1 or 25 ÷
12 = 2 r1.

Pages 20–21
27 ÷ 9 = 3
30 ÷ 3 = 10
18 ÷ 2 = 9
42 ÷ 2 = 21
Home Learn
100 ÷ 2 = 50
50 ÷ 2 = 25
51 ÷ 2 = 25 r 1
11 x 2 = 22
13 ÷ 2 = 6 r1

Pages 22–23
Roger: 42 ÷ 10 = 4 remainder 2
Home Learn
a) 60 carrots (6 x 10)
b) 12 cabbages (120 ÷ 10)
c) 1200 potatoes (120 x 10)

Pages 24–25
The numbers in the 5 Times Table
all end in a 0 or a 5.
The numbers in the 10 Times
Table all end in a 0.

Ladybirds:
There are 3 groups of 5.
If there had been 17 ladybirds,
2 would have been left over.
Home Learn
a) 20 x 5 = 100
b) 90 ÷ 5 = 18
c) 12 x 5 = 60
d) 80 ÷ 5 = 16
e) 60 ÷ 5 = 12

Pages 26–27
300 x 5 = 1500
Home Learn
Stickers: 19 ÷ 3 = 6 r 1
Chocolate coins: 33 ÷ 3 = 11
Felt-tip pens: 17 ÷ 3 = 5 r 2
Micro-robots: 9 ÷ 3 = 3
Louis has: 6 stickers,
11 chocolate coins, 5 felt pens
and 3 micro-robots.
Mrs Campbell has kept back
the remainders: 1 sticker and
2 felt pens.

Pages 28–29
1. Polly has 18 mint Spangles
(3 x 5 = 15   15 + 3 =18)
Jack has 26 mint Spangles
(5 x 5 = 25   25 + 1 = 26)
Keisha 39 has mint Spangles
(7 x 5 = 35   35 + 4 = 39)

2. 825 is a multiple of 3 and
a multiple of 5. True
275 is a multiple of 3 and a multiple of 5. False
All numbers that end in 0 are
multiples of 5. True
A number divided by 5 is half the
size of the same number divided
by 10. False (it is double!)

3.
300 400 500 600 700 800 900
1000

4. Mina feeds Percy 15 times
every week (three times a day
for 5 days = 3 x 5)
The rabbit feed lasts for 100 days
(300 ÷ 3)

5. Penny could buy 4 Universe
bars (4 x 20p = 80p)
Penny could buy 8 liquorice sticks
(8 x 9p = 72p)
Penny could buy 10 chews (6 x 10
= 60p, this leaves 20p for the
Universe bar)
Penny needs £2.00 to buy 10
Universe bars (10 x 20p = £2.00)

Pages 30–31
All the multiples of 8 are also
multiples of 4 and multiples of 2.
The answers in the 4 Times Table
are double those in the 2 Times
Table. That is because 4 is
double 2.
The answers in the 8 Times Table
are double those in the 4 Times
Table.

Multiples of 9:
9 19 27 36 45 54 63 72
81 90

The 11 Times Table
1 x 11 = 11
2 x 11 = 22
3 x 11 = 33
4 x 11 = 44
5 x 11 = 55
6 x 11 = 66
7 x 11 = 77
8 x 11 = 88
9 x 11 = 99
10 x 11 = 110

Home Learn
Complete the following. Try
work out the answers before
checking them in the Times
Table Square on page 17.
3 x 7 = 21
9 x 4 = 36
6 x 7 = 42
6 x 4 = 24
9 x 9 = 81

Pages 32–33
Step six:

```
  480
+  72
  552
```

Home Learn

x	50	1
30	1500	30
8	400	8
	1900	38

1900 + 38 = 1938

Pages 36–37
1.
5: 20, 25, 60, 135, 150, 215
4: 20, 36, 60
9: 36, 81, 135
3: 36, 60, 81, 135, 150

2. 36 x 22 = 792

3. a) 800
b) 500
c) 4000

4. Class 3a: 4 teams of 6
(6 x 4 = 24)
Class 3b: 3 teams of 7
(3 x 7 = 21)
Class 3c: 3 teams of 6 and 1
team of 7
(3 x 6 = 18   18 + 7 = 25)

5. a) 52 ÷ 4 = 13
b) There are no cards left over.

Page 39: Home Learn
a) 546 ÷ 3 = 182
b) 670 ÷ 5 = 134
c) 984 ÷ 6 = 164
d) 917 ÷ 7 = 131

Page 41: Home Learn
1 x 23 = 23
2 x 23 = 46
3 x 23 = 69
4 x 23 = 92
5 x 23 = 115
6 x 23 = 138
7 x 23 = 161
8 x 23 = 184
9 x 23 = 207
10 x 12 = 230

Activity: 6325 ÷ 23 = 275

Page 43: Home Learn

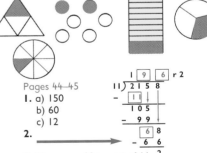

Pages 44–45
1. a) 150
b) 60
c) 12
2.

3. There are 10 teams of 11
(10 x 11 = 110)
a) There are 2 pupils left over
(112 − 110 = 2)
b) 28 oranges are needed
(112 ÷ 4 = 28)
4. a) 180 packs (720 ÷ 4 = 180)
b) 18 boxes (180 ÷ 10 = 18)
c) Twice (18 ÷ 9 = 2)

47

Check Your Progress!